To Renée,

I hope that this book
will help you remember
your visit to Trinity Church
for your book-signing tour!
9 December, 2007

Love, Barbie

CAME THAT THEY MAY
LIFE AND HAVE IT
HE THAT DOETH THE
OF GOD ABIDETH FOREVER

Means *of* Grace, ~ Hope *of* Glory

TRINITY CHURCH
in the City of Boston

IN COMMEMORATION OF
THE 125TH ANNIVERSARY
OF THE CONSECRATION OF
THE CHURCH

This special-edition photoessay was published in commemoration of the 125th anniversary of the consecration of Trinity Church.

Published by Trinity Church in the City of Boston, 545 Boylston Street, Boston MA 02116

The quotation from "Church Going," by Philip Larkin, is reprinted from *The Less Deceived* by permission of The Marvell Press, England and Australia.

Designed, edited, and produced by Vernon Press, Inc., Boston, Massachusetts

Printed in China

Library of Congress Control Card Number 2001095180

CONTENTS

The Hymnal 1982

English poet Philip Larkin, in a poem called "Church Going," describes a casual visitor stopping to look around a church and finding himself asking questions: Why do such places exist? What do they represent? Are they important only for the believers who gather there, or is there something in them for everyone? His final stanza contains these lines:

A serious house on serious earth it is,
In whose blent air all our compulsions meet,
Are recognised, and robed as destinies.
And that much never can be obsolete,
Since someone will for ever be surprising
A hunger in himself to be more serious[.]

For more than 250 years, Trinity Church has provided a "serious house on serious earth" for the city of Boston. Since 1733 people of faith have worshiped at Trinity Church, prayed, listened to sermons there, and gone out to live their faith in Christ-like ways across the city.

In 1871, Trinity parishioners, led by a bold young rector named Phillips Brooks, decided to build a new church in a newly emerging major residential area of the city called the Back Bay. It was a risky endeavor building for a future city only then beginning to emerge, but they were propelled by a determination to articulate and embody a vibrant Christian faith worthy of carrying the people of their city into a new century.

Those were the heady years of Gilded Age prosperity combined with explosive discoveries in science, communications, and technology. A new world was being born. For that world Brooks and the people of Trinity Church were immodest in their aspirations—creating a church with a dramatic design that was at once eclectic and entirely new, thanks to the vision of a brilliant young architect named H.H. Richardson. It was like no other in the United States or indeed anywhere else. They wanted a building at once elegant and intimate, awe-inspiring and humanly embracing—a place where people could be drawn into God's vision for them and the world around them.

Now, 125 years later, set in the heart of Boston's bustling Copley Square, Trinity Church is a revered architectural masterpiece, an icon of Boston's heritage and spirit, but most importantly, a "serious house" for those seeking life's meaning and purpose. Trinity Church today is the spiritual home for a vibrant community of several thousand who come here each week to pray and give thanks, to explore and grow in their faith, and to carry out ministries of service as they work for a world of compassion and justice. But it is also sacred space for the countless visitors from around the world who come here to admire a great work of architecture and, for many, to seek a deeper dimension in their lives. Here many find in the murals and windows, the arches and curves, and the soft, luminous interior light a sense of a deeper dimension, a holy "more" at work in their lives.

As we celebrate the 125th anniversary of this magnificent building, we are keenly aware that Trinity exists for all of these people. A new world is now upon us, perhaps even more so than in the 1870s when the church was built. Faith and spirituality are no longer at the center of contemporary society. Science outstrips our moral capacity to handle what we know. Familiar categories of right and wrong are up for grabs. But what persists is, as Philip Larkin put it, "A hunger . . . to be more serious."

In marking this important milestone in our church's history, we are keenly aware that beautiful architecture, brilliant stained glass windows, and magnificent artwork are powerful tools for the spirit's quest. They invite us to wonder, to reflect on the deeper meaning of our lives. They may in fact lead us into a fresh awareness of the Generous Giver at the heart of the universe whom Christians have met in Jesus Christ.

In this book we hope you will sense a hidden dimension at work not only in this glorious building but also in your life. We hope that the pictures and text will inspire in you a fresh sense of gratitude for the grace and beauty in your own life. And we hope that this building, and the hidden dimension so palpably present in it, will touch those hidden places of longing in your soul with its own hunger to be more serious.

— THE REVEREND SAMUEL T. LLOYD III, RECTOR

YWCA

THE ARCHITECTURE OF TRINITY CHURCH

The spiritual and cultural center of Boston as it appeared in 1900. Trinity Church (1872-77), which commands the east side of Copley Square, faces the Boston Public Library (1888-95), seen at right. The original Museum of Fine Arts (1870-79), at center, stood where the Copley Plaza Hotel now stands. New Old South Meeting House (1872-74) is just out of sight to the right.

In 1885, the *American Architect and Building News* asked its subscribers to name the ten best buildings in the United States. Works by Henry Hobson Richardson took up half the resulting list, and his Trinity Church in the City of Boston, topped the lot. In a similar poll conducted by the *Architectural Record* in 1956, Trinity ranked fourth out of fifty. And in yet another poll on the centenary of the first, a canvass of the Fellows of the American Institute of Architects, Trinity still held its place, at sixth, among the top ten.

Trinity was indeed a standout when new, but what is it about this church that warrants its perennial position among the favorite buildings of American designers, a position it has maintained through more than a century of dramatic changes in the history of architecture? The answer lies in part in its rank as a significant event in the cultural history of the United States, and in part in the coherence and boldness of its design, its fitness to purpose, and the quality of its execution. A comparative glance at Trinity's later neighbors, the neo-Renaissance Boston Public Library and the glassy John Hancock tower, both of which are masterpieces of their eras, quickly demonstrates its timeless distinction.

The design and construction of Trinity Church between 1872 and 1877 launched the career of America's first celebrity architect and coincided with the cultural coming of age of the United States. Richardson was just thirty-three when he entered the competition for the commission. Louisiana-born, a graduate of Harvard, and a student at the École des Beaux-Arts in Paris during the Civil War, he had worked for a short six years in New York drawing parish churches, small houses, and other minor works when his winning design for Trinity projected him onto the national—even international—stage. With the dedication of the building he became this country's most influential builder, our first "signature" architect. The Franco-Spanish Romanesque style he used here for the first time in America evolved into the

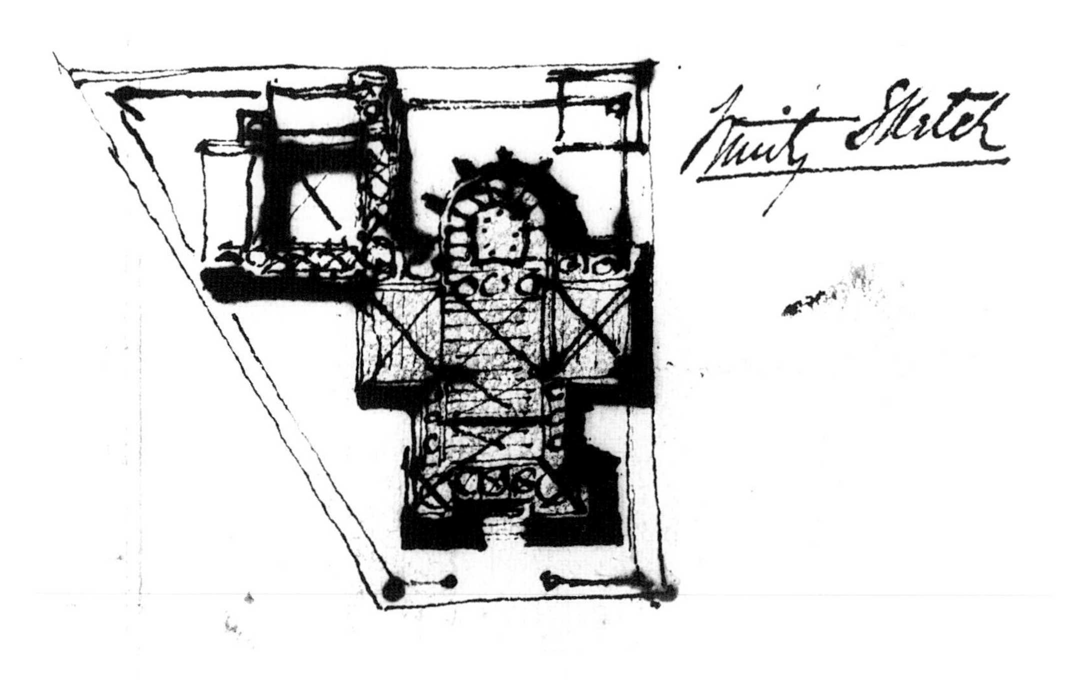

A characteristically bold sketch by H. H. Richardson showing an intermediate cruciform plan for Trinity Church.

"Richardsonian Romanesque." It spread across the country in the hands of other designers, shaping churches, courthouses, libraries, railroad depots, and other buildings for the rest of the century.

But Trinity was more than a personal triumph. It was not only the cornerstone of Richardson's career, it reflected the cultural maturation of America. The church was the work of an architect born in the 1830s who, at Trinity, began to forge a personal architectural language based on, but creatively reinterpreted from, European historical styles. Other artists of his generation were busily forging their own American voices: architects like Frank Furness in Philadelphia, writers like Mark Twain and Emily Dickinson, and painters like Thomas Eakins and Winslow Homer. During the celebration of the centennial of the signing of the Declaration of Independence in the 1870s, these and other artists first created works of recognizably American freshness.

Architectural design is a process of call and response: the call, or requirements, of the client and the response of the designer to those needs. Beyond the general necessities of an ecclesiastical building, Richardson at Trinity sought primarily to give architectural form to the spellbinding preaching of his friend, the Rector Phillips Brooks. When he received the call, the handwritten letter from the Building Committee asking him to join the competition, the architect turned it over and sketched out alternate schemes. One was for the longitudinal nave of three aisles with clerestory that had become characteristic of Gothic Revival Episcopal churches since the formation of the Cambridge Camden Society in England in 1839. These reformers within the church advocated a return to medieval forms of liturgy and specifically Gothic forms of architecture, and they had had a great impact on ecclesiastical design ever since. But a three-aisled nave meant a space intruded upon by piers that would obstruct sight and hearing, and the letter specifically called for "no columns" and "good acoustic qualities."

So the architect next sketched a Greek cross, with chancel, nave, and transepts of equal size grouped around a central square. This foreshadowed an open auditorium plan closer to the dictates of contemporary Congregational practice than current Episcopal design. But then, as in that non-liturgical denomination, the Word, housed in Phillips Brooks's commanding figure and expressed through his shining eyes and resonant voice, was to occupy the center of any service at which he presided. It became the raison d'etre of Richardson's design. That Greek cross sketch formed the embryo that would grow into the great centralized hall that is the essence of Trinity. With one of the arms emphasized for the chancel and the nave slightly deeper than the transepts and flanked by vestigial side aisles, the final plan nodded to Episcopal expectations, but nonetheless created the basis for the great open theater that is the church's interior.

Trinity copied no existing European building, new or old. While Richardson followed nineteenth-century expectations that the church be inspired by medieval work, he chose the substantial Romanesque over the lighter Gothic. The historian can point to forms at Trinity that have precedents in French and Spanish Romanesque buildings, and indeed, the architect himself named the eleventh-century churches of central France as his inspiration, but he called his work a "free rendering" of those sources, and the plan evolved from specifically local requirements. There is no Romanesque church in Europe that has a footprint anything like that of Trinity. Nor was there a European interior that directly foretold the spatial characteristics of this church.

This cutaway perspective of the interior of Trinity Church shows its pyramidal spatial form but not the final design of the overhead wooden vaults.

Rising from Trinity's auditorium plan is a work of conservative technology and traditional materials. The Building Committee contracted with Norcross Brothers of Worcester, Massachusetts, to give three-dimensional form to Richardson's drawings. Then at the beginning of a distinguished career in which he pioneered general contracting in this country, the operative partner, Orlando Whitney Norcross, was to become the architect's frequent collaborator. Norcross's conservative building methods suited Richardson's aims perfectly. The keynote here is Romanesque mass rather than Gothic line, but Romanesque adapted to existing tectonic possibilities. The Romanesque is an arcuated structural style, but large-scale masonry vaults were not yet common in this country. Trinity has wall arches but no structural vault. Load-bearing masonry walls carry the weight of overhead wooden trusses. The wood-and-plaster vaulted shapes that hang from these trusses exert no diagonal thrust so there are no working external buttresses. (Those outside the chancel are there of stylistic choice.) The piers supporting the central tower are founded on massive pyramidal foundations that are themselves resting on piles driven into the soft fill of the Back Bay. This constructional method shaped the interior and the exterior of the church. Questions about the ability of the underlying soil to support the tall tower originally proposed by the architect led to design changes that resulted in the final silhouette.

The apse under construction by Norcross Brothers. As the principal structural system was trabeated rather than vaulted, the buttresses are decorative rather than structurally necessary.

In plan, the central square rises on the interior through corner piers into the broad crossing tower ceiled at the height of some one hundred feet above the floor. Below, the space spreads out between the piers through great arches into the vault-covered chancel, nave, and shallow transepts. Although in plan a longitudinal axis reaches from the western door along the central aisle through the nave and crosses into the chancel, the three-dimensional effect is that of a centralized space rising from the modified cruciform perimeter into the tower. The vast interior is one coherent vessel: open, static, and serene; its cross-section, a pyramid of space.

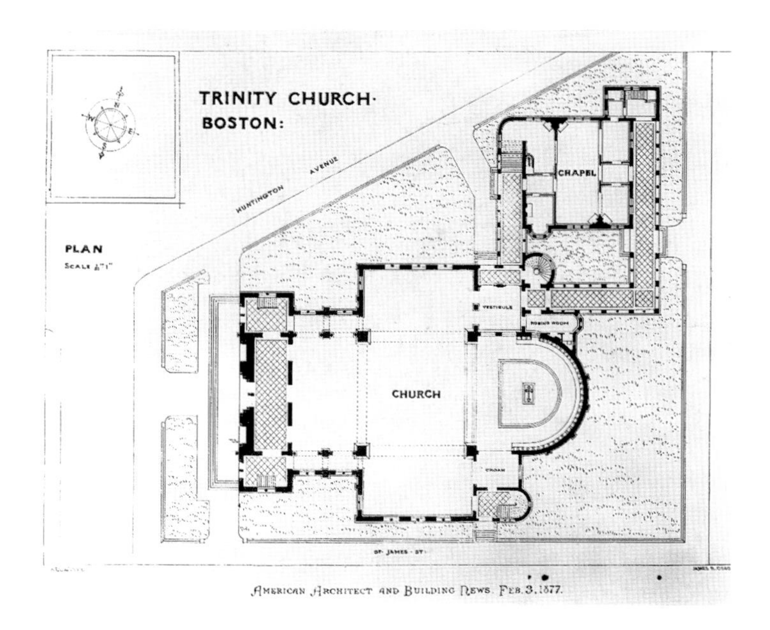

A plan of the church as it appeared at its dedication in 1877.

But Richardson sought more than openness and serenity. "The rich effect of color in the interior was an essential element of the design," he wrote. To make this a reality he persuaded the Building Committee to hire John La Farge of New York to decorate the church. La Farge, a French-trained artist,

At Richardson's urging, Trinity hired John La Farge to decorate the interior of the church with figures from the Old and New testaments.

had no experience in large-scale architectural programs, and few monumental American examples from which to learn. His work at Trinity set the pattern for large-scale mural decoration to come.

With a host of assistants La Farge enriched the prepared deep red walls of the tower with monumental figures of Moses, David, Jeremiah, Isaiah, Paul, Peter, and the Evangelists, as well as Biblical scenes. Not only a major painter of his day, La Farge (with his rival, Louis Comfort Tiffany) also initiated the era of opalescent stained glass in this country, and he eventually supplied designs for windows in the north transept and nave. Other glasswork came from a variety of designers. The chancel windows were made by the English firm of Clayton and Bell; William Morris and Edward Burne-Jones provided glass in the baptistry and north transept. Some of the windows of the south transept are the work of A. Oudinot of Paris; others were made by Cottier & Co. of New York. The unity of Richardson's space embraces them all.

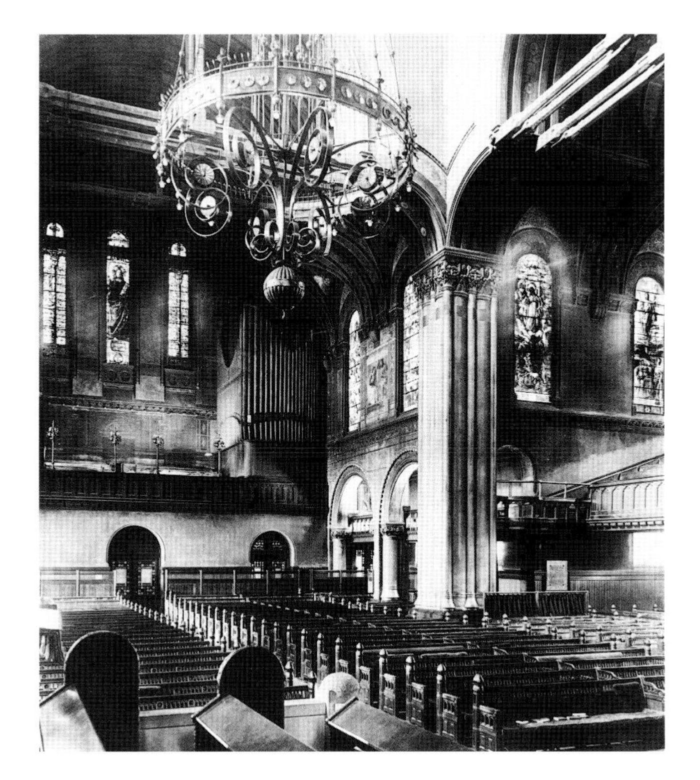

Looking west from the chancel, with John La Farge's tripartite window, *Christ in Majesty,* above the western entrance. The glorious chandelier, or "corona," visible here, was later removed as part of a renovation.

It is not so much in its details—although they are indeed artistically fine—as in its overall architectural impact that the work of La Farge and other decorators adds to Richardson's Trinity. As Phillips Brooks delivered his sermons from a pulpit that was originally near the center of the chancel entrance, he could be seen and heard from every pew in the vast hall. As he preached he could look for inspiration to La Farge's tripartite *Christ in Majesty* glowing opposite him above the entrance, the translucent figure rising resplendent against the western light flanked by lancets of voluptuous aquamarine. This is without doubt the single most stunning example of glasswork in America. But it is in its totality that Trinity's interior affects the worshipper most. In the end, with the open space surrounded by the ruddy, figured walls, the colorful geometric patterns of the overhead barrel shapes, and the luminous stained glass, the architect conceived—and the multitude of designers achieved—one of the simplest and yet richest ecclesiastical interiors in American architecture.

Although it has changed a bit since Richardson's day, Trinity still ranks among the most inspired and moving sacred spaces in the country, if not the world. The chancel furniture dates from the mid-twentieth century and the present pulpit was added in 1916. But the gravest change occurred with the removal of the wrought-iron chandelier, or "corona," that once gave scale to the vast interior beneath the tower. Despite these alterations the interior remains the essence of Trinity. Its true quality is seen when the electric lighting is switched off, and colored daylight streaming through the western lancets and other stained glass windows falls upon and reflects from the colorful walls, suffusing the interior. Then the broad, serene, hushed space seems

Trinity Church under construction (foreground), with the New Old South Meeting House rising at the corner of Boylston and Dartmouth streets (background).

Before the modern transformation of Copley Square, Trinity was more tightly bounded by city streets than it is today. Richardson responded to the free-standing site by creating a pyramidal composition that is effective from all sides.

physically palpable. Without harsh modern illumination, color and shadow saturate the room, filling the void. Deep organ tones add aural enhancement to the visual experience. This was the architectural impact sought by Richardson. At the time of the dedication the *Boston Evening Transcript* remarked on its "solidity and grandeur of effect not to be described, but to be seen and felt."

On the exterior the plan rises into a pyramidal form that encloses and is shaped by that grand interior space. We are reminded by the quiet voice of Richardson's slightly older Massachusetts contemporary, Amherst's Emily Dickinson, that "the Outer—from the Inner/Derives its Magnitude." Trinity's centralized plan and pyramidal interior give the exterior its majestic presence.

As with the plan, the interior and exterior of a mid-nineteenth-century Episcopal church might have been expected to follow Gothic Revival precedent. Such a church would have been long and tall, with thin walls opened by pointed arches, rich in delicate detail, and with a tower and spire centered on or set to one side of its western front. This would have produced an asymmetrical, picturesque silhouette akin to that of Cummings and Sears's New Old South Meeting House that rose contemporary with Trinity on the corner of Boylston and Dartmouth streets. Richardson wanted none of that. His site was a free-standing one, surrounded by streets on all four sides, and the church was thus to be seen in the round. He admired the sturdy lithic masses, round-arched openings, and centered silhouettes of the Romanesque churches of central France. In the

Auvergne, he wrote, “the tower became, as it were, the Church, and the composition took the outline of a pyramid, the apse, transepts, nave and chapels forming only the base to the obelisk of the tower.” Such a relationship of parts exactly suited the site and the auditorium plan suggested by the requirements of Trinity’s Building Committee.

So he made the central tower the main feature of his exterior, reducing the twin western towers to mere antecedents. Richardson originally wanted a taller one, but eventually lowered and reworked it after an example on the Romanesque Old Cathedral at Salamanca in Spain. Its central position eliminated the splintering effect, the “struggle for precedence,” as he also wrote, between a church and its asymmetrical spire. A church that becomes its spire is a unified composition.

Trinity rises like a mountain of masonry from the city streets, a balanced, static mass of stone, radiating permanence, order, dignity, stability, and repose. This was more evident before the richly carved western porch and flanking turrets were added in the

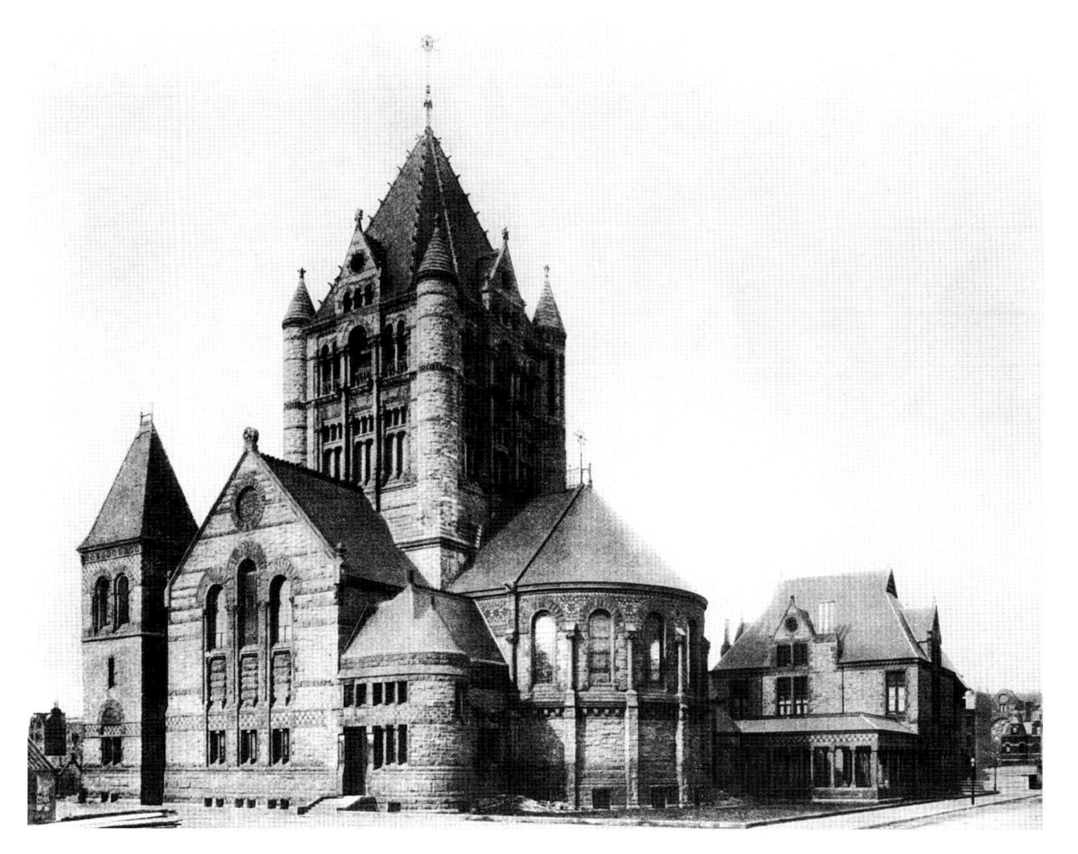

A view of Trinity Church from the east, showing the pyramidal composition of apse, transepts, and central tower. The silhouette was inspired by the Romanesque churches of the Auvergne in France; the tower by one on the Old Cathedral at Salamanca in Spain.

The church in the late 1880s. Richardson's designs for the western towers and entrance porch were never realized. The existing elaborate additions were designed by and erected under the supervision of his successors in the 1890s.

1890s by his successors, the architectural firm of Shepley, Rutan and Coolidge. The porch is a superbly wrought design, but one that closely follows its precedent at St. Gilles-du-Gard in Provence. Its multitudinous figures (including Phillips Brooks, one of at least four likenesses of the preacher to be found in and around the building) introduced a note of busy detail to a church that did not require it. Elsewhere in the church, Richardson was inspired by the general rather than the specific characteristics of his sources. As the architect said, "the distinguishing characteristics of a style are independent of details," and this was especially true of the Romanesque, "which in its treatment of masses, affords an inexhaustible source of study quite independent of its merits as a school of sculpture." At Trinity, as in his other mature works, Richardson created a building with a minimum of carved ornament. He composed it of large exterior masses of masonry that are themselves sculpted by light and shadow.

In Richardson's work at Trinity, ornamental detail gave way to elemental architectural concerns, such as the use of first-class building materials; solid construction; the relationships between mass and void and of the building to its site; the expression of shelter; and the roles of color, texture, scale, and style. The architect chose Romanesque for its "grandeur and repose." Whereas the Gothic is a skeletal style of piers and glass, the Romanesque is an architecture of heavy masonry; the former is pinched, the latter, generous. In choosing the Romanesque the architect sought a "quiet and massive treatment of wall surfaces." To give substance to Richardson's design Norcross opened quarries for sandstone and granite at Longmeadow and Dedham, Massachusetts, and Westerly, Rhode Island. The contractor's workmen characteristically created stonework of the highest craftsmanship. The exterior walls are of rock-faced granite laid up in a random ashlar pattern set in red mortar. Belt courses, the frames of openings, and carved details are of sandstone. In an era when polychromy was the hallmark of fashionable architecture, with arches and other details compounded of contrasting stones, Richardson reduced his palate to two colors and his arches to monochromatic curves of sandstone blocks. This restrained

"The struggle for precedence, which often takes place between a Church and its spire, was disposed of, by at once and completely subordinating nave, transepts, and apse, and grouping them about the tower as the central mass."
—*From H. H. Richardson's "Description of Trinity Church," 1877.*

chromatic selection reinforced the overall static composition, and enhanced the sense of muscular quietude that characterizes the exterior of the church.

At the same time, the dance of light and shadow across the rock-faced stones animates the surfaces of the exterior. Such vivacity prevents the building's external image from going stale, as does Richardson's characteristic interplay of symmetry and asymmetry, which occurs in the details as in the whole. The turrets at the corners of the main tower seem identical at first glance, but that to the northeast rises higher than the rest, has windows, and contains a stairway that is clearly expressed by the stepped molding in the stonework of the exterior. On the Clarendon Street elevation of the chapel, the composition balanced around the axis rising from the center of the ground floor arcade through the muntin of the second floor window and the dormer above is upset by a closed bay added to the north and a colonnade to the south. And finally, the balanced main mound of the church is offset by the smaller, asymmetrically placed chapel at the corner of Boylston and Clarendon. At the beginning of his career Richardson announced his search for a "bold, rich, living architecture," and at Trinity he first achieved his goal.

Richardson vitalized his designs in many ways, including here the play of symmetry and asymmetry on the eastern façade of the chapel (later remodeled to serve as the parish house).

Copley Square in the late 1880s. Seen here are the porch of New Old South Meeting House (foreground), Trinity without its entrance porch or western towers, and the original Museum of Fine Arts (right). Trinity's sturdy proportions set it apart from the brittleness of its Victorian Gothic neighbors.

Richardson lived just nine years after the dedication of the church, yet he left an indelible mark on the history of American architecture. He went on from Trinity to create memorable designs for commuter railroad stations, small town libraries, residences, the New York State Senate chamber in Albany, the Marshall Field Wholesale Store in Chicago, and the Allegheny County Court House in Pittsburgh. Most of the characteristics of his mature style occur at Trinity. Not only did his signature Romanesque vocabulary first appear here, but also evident are such timeless characteristics as his ability to get the best out of his collaborators; the demand for excellent craftsmanship; his controlled yet enlivened forms; the studied relationship of part to part, window to wall, roof to mass, inside to outside, and space to space; his use of and respect for the properties of natural materials; weight, measure, and grounded proportions; the sense of shelter and of authority; and of, finally, the church as a "mighty fortress." In his reworking of traditional forms and materials Richardson refreshed the best of the past for the problems of his time, and in so doing he created a work still considered a masterpiece 125 years later.

In the small cloister off Clarendon Street, on the exterior wall of the chancel, there is a tablet dedicated to Richardson's memory. It was put in place by Boston architects in 1913. For all of his later achievements, it remembers this as "his noblest work." But Trinity Church is more than that: it remains one of the nation's noblest architectural achievements.

—JAMES F. O'GORMAN

Consecrated space, holy words, hallowed gestures, sacred songs—these are some of the resources that the human spirit has gathered into the treasury of worship. Deep within the human heart still stirs the spirit of wonder and awe, the spirit that cries "Holy!" whenever it stands before the transcendently beautiful, the ultimately good, the supremely true, wherever it finds them. Church buildings and liturgies and songs are raised to offer glimpses of that wonder and awe. As we celebrate the 125th anniversary of the dedication of the consecrated space that enfolds our worship, we do so in a spirit of thanksgiving for all that is gracious and glorious in our lives—of which this remarkable building is a sign, symbol, and icon.

The integrity of a vessel, says an old Japanese proverb, is the space that it contains. So it is with H.H. Richardson's Trinity Church on Copley Square. Solid walls, foursquare and massive on the outside, towering to a great height, dissolve in the interior to a gentle embracing frame, to hold—as if in the palm of a loving mother's hand—a worshipping people. Colorful windows, striking murals, and rich stencil patterns all fade away, serving the purpose for which they were intended: to lift a people's prayers and the people themselves into the very reality of God's amazing grace. No more than a setting for a great gem can compete with its beauty, Trinity Church serves the people it houses and the God they worship, rendering them a fragrant sacrifice, holy and acceptable, and giving them glimpses of hope and glory.

This vast and noble space, designed in the first place as a room for great preaching, is no less intimate and engaging for all its grandeur and scale. The great curved wall of the apse turns the arms of its Greek cross into an embrace that includes everyone. The chancel, as Phillips Brooks and H.H. Richardson conceived of it, carries the intimacy around the Word preached up to the table where the Sacrament is celebrated. There is space enough to hint at God's infinitude, but also space enough for every worshipper to enter into the rituals of prayer and praise. No mere spectators here, rather all are participants in the drama of salvation that is about them and the story of their lives. It is easy to forget that one may have entered as a visitor yet found in the building's own witness and welcome that one is not "a stranger or a guest, but like a child at home."

We gather every Sunday at Trinity to give thanks. Above all else, it is a spirit of thanksgiving that lies at the heart of Christian worship. This understanding of heart-felt gratitude in response to a bounteous God is part of the priceless legacy we have inherited from our Jewish ancestors in the faith. God is good—and for this we can do no other than give thanks, when circumstances are agreeable and when challenges abound on every side. Life is God's gift and thus is good—and for this we cannot help but give thanks at all of life's great moments of passage, as much at a long-expected birth as at a grievous loss through a tragic death. God is merciful and forgiving—and for this we cannot help but give thanks, when the stains of our sins are washed clean away, and the fetters that shackle us to our private captivities are shattered. We raise

our hearts and voices to take up the song of the Psalmist to sing with Jews and Christians in every age and time: Let us give thanks to the Lord, for God's mercy endures forever.

The Holy Eucharist is a thanksgiving prayer, the word *eucharist* being derived from the Greek *eucharisto,* which means to give thanks. In our worship, first and foremost, we give thanks for all things great and small, and especially for the mighty acts by which God creates, redeems, and makes us holy. No one is too small or too great to offer the sincere words of a grateful heart. The original phrasing of *The General Thanksgiving,* so beloved of Episcopalians, is believed by many to have been suggested by a private prayer of Elizabeth I, issued in 1596:

> I render unto thee, O merciful and heavenly Father, most humble and hearty thanks for thy manifold mercies so abundantly bestowed upon me, as well as for my creation, preservation, regeneration, and all the other thy benefits and great mercies exhibited in Christ Jesus.

These words from the grateful heart of a great queen have inspired the prayers of many other grateful hearts since they were first issued more than four hundred years ago. It is, however, something of an irony that this prayer of royal origin became especially familiar to American worshipers as a result of the American Revolution. With the dispersal of the loyalist clergy in the wake of independence, the church that would become the Episcopal Church soon had little access to the Eucharist, and it was *The General Thanksgiving* in the Daily Office that served to lift the prayers of thankful hearts to God. The regular, weekly repetition of this prayer, led by lay people from the midst of the people, has significantly shaped the tradition of public prayer and praise that we know as Episcopalian.

The revisers of *The Book of Common Prayer 1789*, the first American version, moved *The General Thanksgiving* from the Occasional Prayers, making it part of the regular corporate worship of the Daily Office. There for the last two hundred years it has remained, a signpost to guide the people's prayers, a pathway along which to approach the God of grace and in which to learn the lessons that make a heart sing with grateful praise.

The revision of *The Book of Common Prayer* in 1892 allowed its omission except on Sundays and feastdays when the Holy Eucharist was not celebrated immediately following the Daily Office. The 1928 edition follows the Irish revision of 1877, which allowed the congregation to say the prayer along with the minister. The present edition directs that the prayer be said by officiant and people.

To say this prayer, and to say it regularly, is to keep in constant focus God's threefold activity as Creator, Preserver, and Redeemer, and never to forget how great a blessing is our creation, preservation, and redemption. Perhaps, most memorably, God's redemption of the world through the action of Jesus Christ is expressed in the unforgettable phrase "the means of grace and the hope of glory"[from the pen of Bishop Edward Reynolds of Norwich, a low-churchman with Puritan sympathies who adapted the prayer for inclusion in the 1662 *Book of Common Prayer*]. We hear in these words the echoes of Paul's theology of grace, in which God "makes known the riches of the glory of this mystery, which is Christ in you, the hope of glory." [Colossians 1:27]

Grateful hearts inspire grateful lives, and grateful lives praise God in word and deed, proclaiming and showing forth a thankful spirit in all that is said and in everything that is done. The eloquent and earnest cadences of *The General Thanksgiving* teach us that gratitude is the mother of service and thanksgiving the father of self-sacrifice. Holiness and righteousness that will continue all our days are the fruits that grow from the seeds of thankfulness, rather than the stern results of austere discipline and strict duty.

The final petition of the prayer is undergirded and sustained by words familiar to worshipers, who, finding them here, catch glimpses of the continuing worship of the church in which they are privileged to share. From the *Miserere mei* [Psalm 51] comes the versicle that launches the Daily Office and whose response finds an echo here: "Open my lips O Lord,* and my mouth shall *show forth your praise."* So, too, the words of the Benedictus [Luke 1:68–79], with its promise of the Savior's liberating love, inform the gratitude the prayer inspires: "Free to worship him without fear,* *holy and righteous* in his sight, *all the days of our life."*

The General Thanksgiving gives the Daily Office a concluding eucharistic note. Like the Postcommunion Prayer in the Holy Eucharist, it directs our worship in the sanctuary to the tasks of service in the world. It relates our daily prayers to our daily lives by linking the due service of lips to the dutiful service of deeds.

In our lives the Lord God has acted, and it is marvelous in our eyes. As our eyes see the astounding acts by which God creates us and empowers us, hears our prayers and sets us free, finds us and loves us, forgives us and saves us—so our hearts overflow with a profound gratitude that sings, in sighs too deep for words, prayers of eternal thankfulness and praise.

—THE REVEREND BRUCE W. B. JENNEKER, ASSOCIATE RECTOR

THE GENERAL THANKSGIVING

Almighty God, Father of all mercies,
we your unworthy servants give you humble thanks
for all your goodness and loving-kindness
to us and to all whom you have made.

~

We bless you for our creation, preservation,
and all the blessings of this life;
but above all for your immeasurable love
in the redemption of the world by our Lord Jesus Christ;
for the means of grace, and for the hope of glory.

~

And, we pray, give us such an awareness of your mercies,
that with truly thankful hearts we may show forth your praise,
not only with our lips, but in our lives,
by giving up our selves to your service,
and by walking before you
in holiness and righteousness all our days;
through Jesus Christ our Lord,
to whom, with you and the Holy Spirit,
be honor and glory throughout all ages. Amen.

35

36

ADVANCEMENT OF LEARNING A·D·MDCCCLXXXVIII

FedEx
FedEx

ALMIGHTY GOD,

FATHER OF ALL MERCIES,

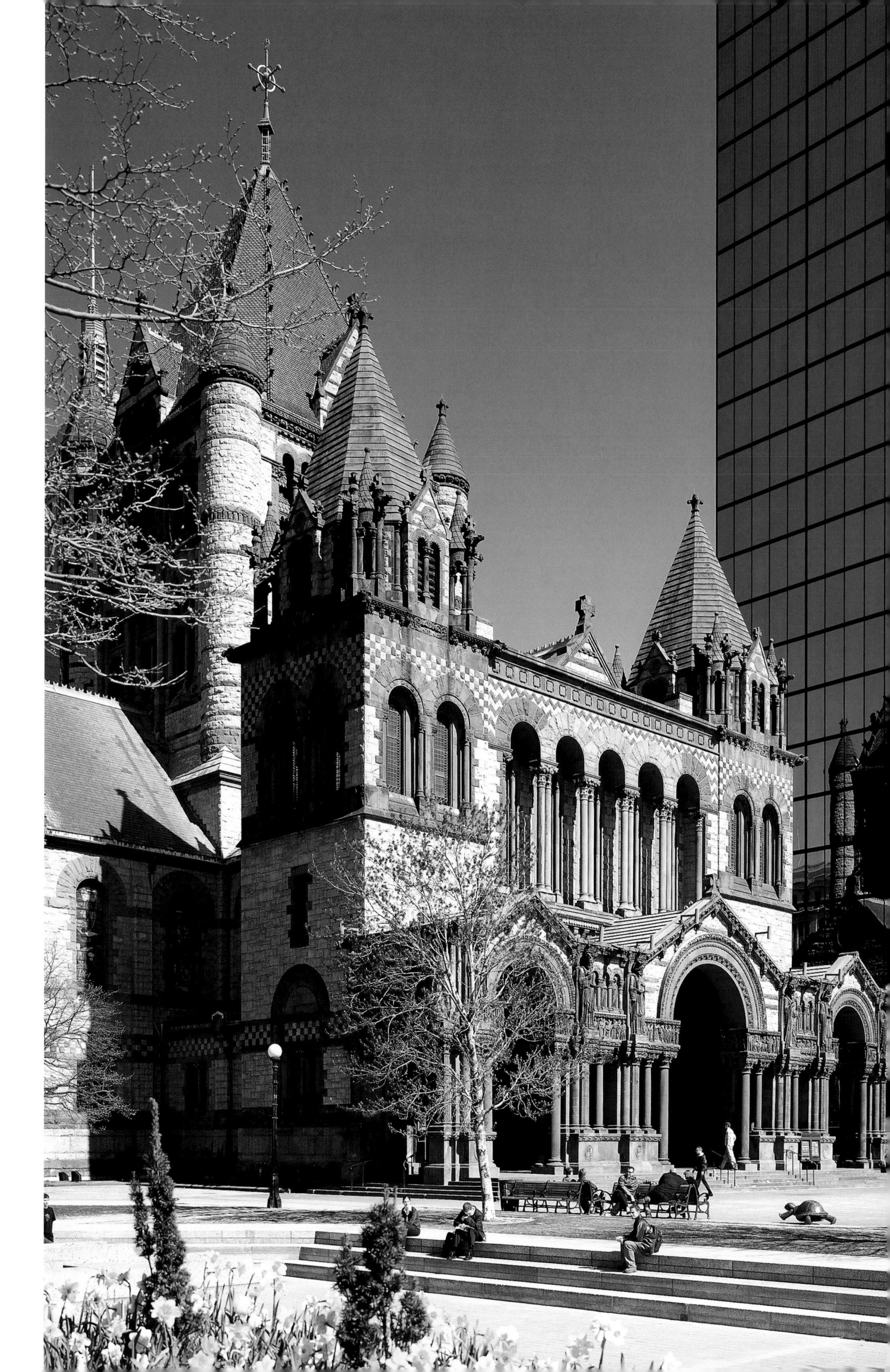

WE YOUR UNWORTHY SERVANTS

GIVE YOU HUMBLE THANKS

44

CLARENDON ST
ST. JAMES AVE
TOW ZONE
NO STOPPING ANY TIME
FedEx

FOR ALL YOUR
GOODNESS AND
LOVING-KINDNESS
TO US AND TO
ALL WHOM YOU
HAVE MADE.

WE BLESS YOU

FOR OUR CREATION, PRESERVATION,

AND ALL THE BLESSINGS OF THIS LIFE; BUT

ABOVE ALL FOR YOUR IMMEASURABLE LOVE

SAMUEL
DAVID
SOLOMON
DANIEL
ABRAHAM
MOSES

IN THE REDEMPTION
OF THE WORLD
BY OUR LORD JESUS CHRIST;

BLESSING AND HONOUR AND GLORY

FOR THE MEANS OF GRACE,

AND FOR THE HOPE OF GLORY.

The Hymnal 1982
The Hymnal 1982
The Hymnal 1982
The Hymnal 1982
The Hymnal 1982
The Hymnal 1982
CATHERINE JANE BRATTON
HOLY BAPTISM
JANUARY 9, 2000
ROBERT + STACY MAGINN
JULY 4, 1987
SEMPER UBIQUE
RICHARD MICHAEL MERRILL

3rd SUN • EASTER
199
195
182

ROBERT TREAT PAINE
CLASSMATE AND FRIEND
OF PHILLIPS BROOKS
VESTRYMAN AND WARDEN
OF THIS PARISH
1874 TO 1910
TO THE GREAT PREACHER
HE GAVE THE FRIENDSHIP
OF A LIFETIME
TO THE PARISH
HE RENDERED LOYAL
AND GENEROUS SERVICE
TO THE GLORY OF GOD
AND IN LOVING MEMORY
OF THEIR FATHER
HIS CHILDREN ERECT
THIS PULPIT

AND, WE PRAY,

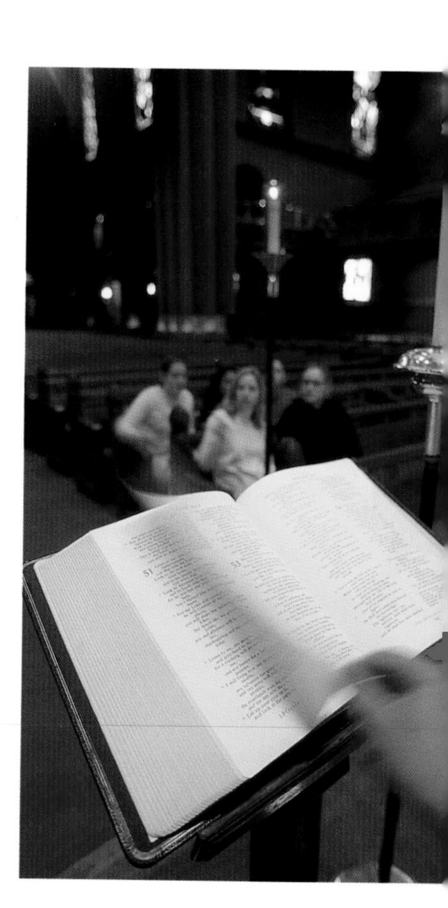

GIVE US SUCH AN AWARENESS

OF YOUR MERCIES,

THAT WITH TRULY THANKFUL HEARTS

THE TRVTH AND
MAKE YOV FREE
HE THAT LOVETH NOT: KNOWETH
NOT GOD: FOR GOD IS LOVE
SEEK YE FIRST THE KINGDOM OF
GOD AND HIS RIGHTEOVSNESS
AND THE WORD WAS MADE
FLESH AND DWELT AMONG VS
ONE LORD ONE FAITH ONE
ONE GOD AND FATHER OF

WE MAY SHOW FORTH
YOUR PRAISE,

HE THAT DOETH THE WILL
OF GOD ABIDETH FOREVER
YE SHALL KNOW THE TRVTH AND
THE TRVTH SHALL MAKE YOV FREE
E THAT LOVETH NOT KNOWE
NOT GOD : FOR GOD IS LOV
ST JOHN
ST LUKE
ST MARK
ST MATTHEW

EK YE FIRST THE KINGDOM OF
D AND HIS RIGHTEOVSNESS
AND THE WORD WAS MADE
FLESH AND DWELT AMONG VS

ST. JOHN
ST. MARK
ST. MATTHEW
YE SHALL KNOW THE TRVTH AND THE TRVTH SHALL MAKE YOV FREE
HE THAT LOVETH NOT: KNOWETH NOT GOD: FOR GOD IS LOVE
SEEK YE FIRST THE KINGDOM OF GOD AND HIS RIGHTEOVSNESS

90

UPON THE
UNTO THE

NOT ONLY WITH OUR LIPS,

BUT IN OUR LIVES,

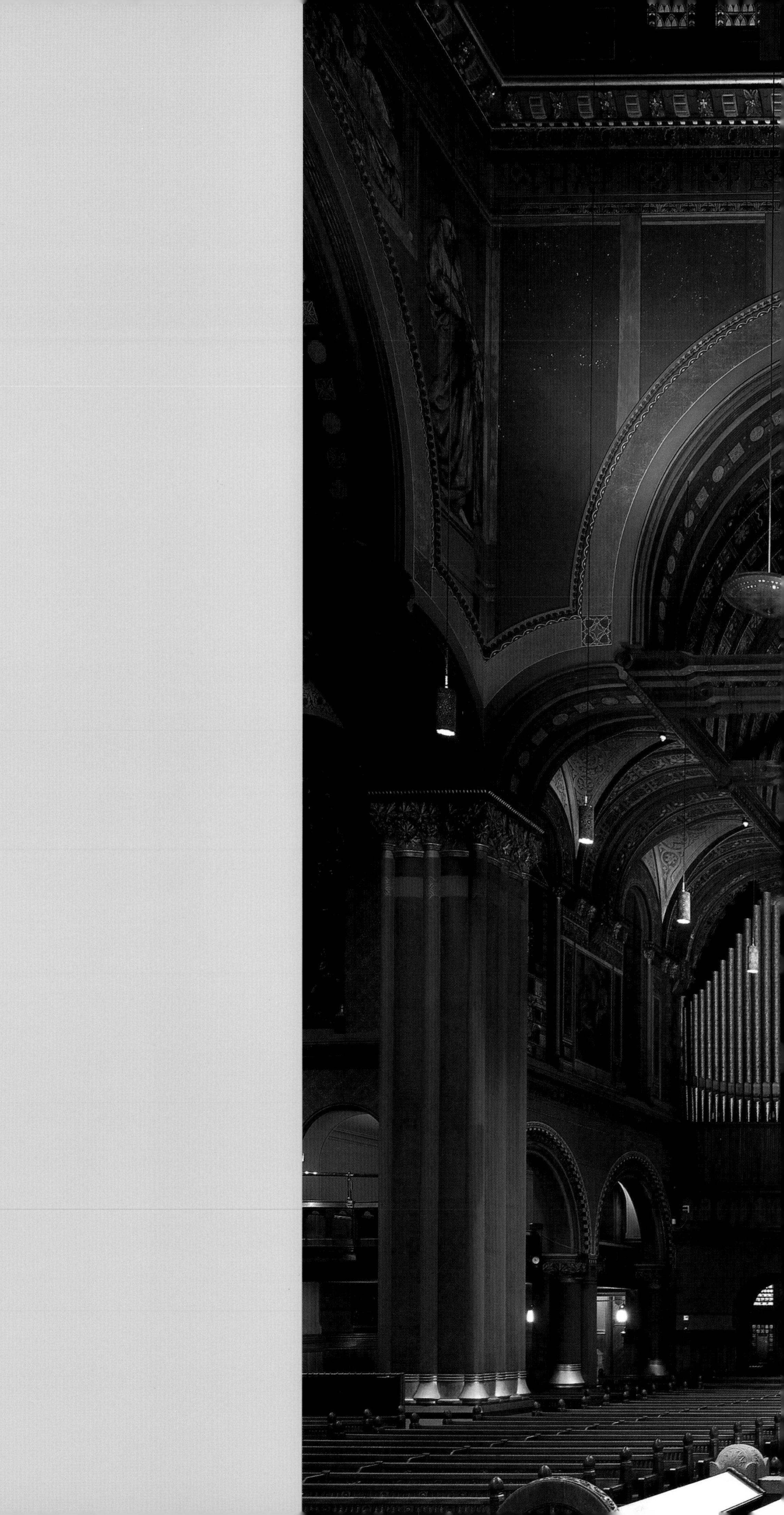

BY GIVING UP OUR SELVES TO YOUR

SERVICE, AND BY WALKING BEFORE YOU

TO GIVE
A RANSOM
HIS LIFE
FOR MANY

100

GIVE
FOR MANY

BROOKS
OF TRINITY CHURCH
A.D. 1869–1891
OF MASSACHUSETTS
A.D. 1891–1893
FULL OF FAITH
OF THE HOLY GHOST

IN HOLINESS

AND RIGHTEOUSNESS ALL OUR DAYS;

112

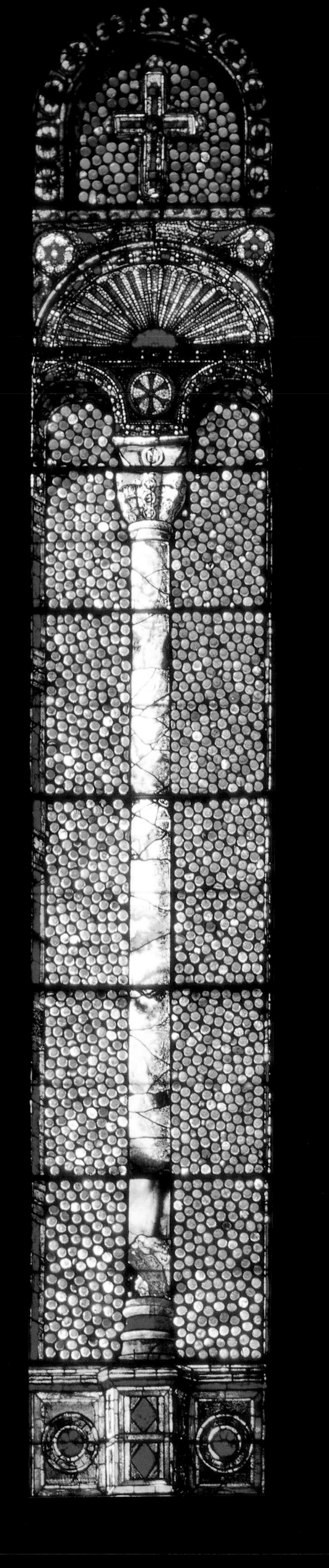

THROUGH
JESUS CHRIST
OUR LORD,
TO WHOM,
WITH YOU
AND THE
HOLY SPIRIT,

BE HONOR AND GLORY

THROUGHOUT ALL AGES.

HE THAT DOETH THE WILL OF GOD ABIDETH FOREVER
YE SHALL KNOW THE TRVTH AND THE TRVTH SHALL MAKE YOV FREE

SEEK YE FIRST THE KINGDOM OF GOD AND HIS RIGHTEOVSNESS
AND THE WORD WAS MADE FLESH AND DWELT AMONG US

AMEN

LIST OF ILLUSTRATIONS

Key to photographers:
[AG] Anton Grassl
[LJ] Lou Jones
[PV] Peter Vanderwarker

5. Children gather for a Good Friday program [LJ]
6. At the communion rail [LJ]

Page 27 Interior detail, staircase and candelabrum [AG]

Page 29 Interior, southeast view [AG]

Page 30 After daily worship [LJ]

Page 31 A welcome from the eagle lectern [LJ]

Page 32 Interior detail, *Chi-Rho* from *Christ in Majesty* window (John La Farge) [AG]

Page 33 Interior detail, chancel vault decoration [AG]

Page 34–35 A bird's-eye view of Trinity Church, facing west [PV]

Pages 36–37 View of Copley Square from central tower [PV]

Page 38 Central tower with John Hancock tower in background [AG]

Page 39 Exterior detail, south transept [PV]

Pages 40–41: Exterior details, porch carvings (left to right)
1. Center arch [AG]
2. St. John [AG]
3. St. Paul and St. Augustine [AG]
4. *Jesus Blessing the Children* [PV]
5. *The Last Supper* [AG]
6. Cross atop center arch [AG]

Page 42 Exterior view, from Copley Square [PV]

Page 43 Exterior view, the Copley Square porch steps at noontime [PV]

Pages 44–45 Exterior view, from Boylston Street [AG]

Pages 46–47 Exterior view, from east [PV]

Page 48 Exterior detail, steps to mezzanine level (formerly a chapel) [AG]

Page 49 Exterior detail, cloister [AG]

Pages 50–51: Exterior details, cloister (left to right)
1. Stonework [AG]
2. Column base [AG]

3. St. Francis statue, the garth garden [AG]
4. Door stop, Clarendon Street entrance [AG]
5. Columns with capitals [AG]
6. Steps to mezzanine level (formerly a chapel) [PV]

Pages 52–53 Window tracery given as a friendship gift by the Church of St. Botolph, Boston, England [AG]

Pages 54–55 Exterior detail, cloister and garth garden [AG]

Pages 56–57 Exterior detail, cloister and garth garden at night [AG]

Page 58 Exterior detail, St. Francis statue, the garth garden [PV]

Page 59 Exterior detail, fountain in the garth garden, looking toward Phillips Brooks office [AG]

Pages 60–61 Exterior views of the porch: (Left) winter; (Center and Right) spring [PV]

Page 62 Exterior detail, carvings on north-porch façade: Heroes of the Old Testament (Left to Right, Abraham, Samuel, David, Solomon, Daniel, Elijah, Moses) [AG]

Page 63 Exterior view, porch at night [PV]

Page 64 Interior detail, decorative support for chancel cross [AG]

Page 65 Interior view, the chancel as seen from the Copley Square vestibule [PV]

Page 66 Interior detail, staircase and candelabrum as seen from the Copley Square vestibule [PV]

Page 67 Interior detail, column and arches [PV]

Page 68 Interior view, central tower and chancel [PV]

Page 69 Interior detail, chancel above nun's gallery [AG]

Page 70 Interior view, gallery in north transept [PV]

Page 71 Interior detail, *The Resurrection* window (John La Farge) [PV]

Page 72 Interior detail, choir pews in chancel [AG]

Page 73 Interior detail, commemorative kneelers [AG]

Page 74 A view from the balcony during a service [LJ]

Page 75 Interior view, pulpit and gallery in south transept [PV]

Pages 76–77 Interior detail, carvings on the pulpit built in memory of Robert Treat Paine, 1916: (left to right) St. Paul, St. Chrysostom, Nativity scene, Martin Luther [PV]

Pages 78–79 Interior view, pulpit canopy, transept and chancel ceiling, central tower [PV]

Page 80 (Left) Setting the altar for the Great Thanksgiving [LJ]
(Right) Reading the lesson at daily worship [LJ]

Page 81 (Left) A Good Friday *Stations of the City* walk along Boston Common [LJ]
(Right) Filling the font at baptism [LJ]

Page 82 (Left) Eucharistic bread and wine [LJ] (Right) At the communion rail [LJ]

Page 83 (Left) Children in the chancel [LJ] (Right) A lay reader at the eagle lectern [LJ]

Page 84 Interior view, pulpit and chancel [PV]

Page 85 Interior detail, carving on the Rector's stall [PV]

Pages 86–87 Interior view, the chancel [AG]

Page 88 Interior detail, the chancel cross [AG]

Page 89 Interior detail, the chancel [PV]

Page 90 Interior detail, the eagle lectern [AG]

Page 91 Interior view, from the organ console [PV]

Page 92 Children's Choir [LJ]

Page 93 (Left) At the organ [LJ] (Right) The choir singing an anthem [LJ]

Pages 94–95 Interior view, west wall [PV]

Page 96 (Left) After the service [LJ] (Right) At the communion rail [LJ]

Page 97 Closing procession [LJ]

Page 98 Interior detail, chancel wall above the nun's gallery [AG]

Page 99 Interior detail, balcony in north transept [AG]

Page 100 Interior detail, ceiling decoration and window [AG]

Page 101 Interior detail, gallery in south transept [PV]

Page 102 Interior detail, looking through the chancel into the baptistery [PV]

Page 103 Interior detail, baptismal font and Phillips Brooks bust by Daniel Chester French [PV]

Pages 104–105: stained-glass window details (left to right)
1. *David's Charge to Solomon* (Burne-Jones & Morris) [PV]
2. *David's Charge to Solomon* (Burne-Jones & Morris) [PV]
3. *David's Charge to Solomon* (Burne-Jones & Morris) [PV]
4. *Charity (The Good Samaritan)* (Burlison & Grills of London) [PV]
5. *David's Charge to Solomon* (Burne-Jones & Morris) [PV]

Pages 106–107 Interior detail, the baptistery [PV]

Page 108 (all) At the organ [AG]

Page 109 Interior view, organ pipes, west entrance [PV]

Pages 110–111 Interior detail, organ pipes [AG]

Page 112 Interior detail, organ pipes [PV]

Page 113 Interior detail, organ pipes [AG]

Pages 114–115 Interior detail, *Christ in Majesty* window (John La Farge) [PV]

Page 116 (Left) A flower-guild member at work [LJ] (Right) Sunday service [LJ]

Page 117 (Left) Parent and child [LJ] (Right) Acolyte preparing for a service [LJ]

Pages 118–119 Reading the Passion Gospel on Palm Sunday [PV]

Page 120 Interior detail, entrance off Copley Square [PV]

Page 121 After the service [PV]

Page 128 At the foot of Phillips Brooks statue by Augustus Saint-Gaudens [AG]

DESIGNED BY
PETER M. BLAIWAS
FOR VERNON PRESS, INC.

COMPOSITION SET IN
SCALA AND SCALA SANS
BY DIX! QUALITY GRAPHICS

PRODUCTION SUPERVISION
BY SUSAN MCNALLY

PRINTED AND BOUND
IN CHINA BY
ASIA PACIFIC OFFSET, INC.